NO LONGER PROPERTY OF
SEATTLE PUBLIC LIBRARY

Poems about Dads

My Daddy Rules the World

poems and illustrations by

Hope Anita Smith

Christy Ottaviano Books

HENRY HOLT AND COMPANY
NEW YORK

MY DADDY

My daddy is a porcupine
with whiskers that are prickly.

My daddy is an octopus
who finds where I am tickly.

My daddy is a tall giraffe
who lifts me to the sky.

My daddy is a sea eagle
who teaches me to fly.

My daddy is a wise old owl
who stays up late at night.

My daddy is a big brown bear
with arms that hug me tight.

WHEN DADDY IS SLEEPING

When Daddy is sleeping
I don't make a sound.
My feet are like feathers
when they hit the ground.

My laugh is so quiet.
And so is my roar.
And so is the way
that I close the back door.

When Daddy is sleeping
I whisper to talk.
I chew with my mouth closed.
I tiptoe to walk.

I'm as quiet as a rabbit,
as a turtle or a fish.
I'm as quiet as a dream
or a real birthday wish.

But when Daddy is sleeping
he isn't quiet.
He makes a noise
that's as loud as a riot!

It sounds just like horses
galloping fast,
getting louder and louder
as they rumble past.

I have a drum set
and a real horn that blows,
but Daddy is loudest
when he plays
his nose!

TABLE FOR TWO

My daddy makes me breakfast
on Sundays when I wake—
hot cereal, fresh orange juice,
and muffins, if he bakes.
Everyone's still sleeping
except Daddy and me.
We eat, we talk, we laugh a lot,
and I'm so glad to be
having breakfast with my daddy—
all by myself, just me.

LOVE LETTER

My daddy—
he is far away.
I write to him
most every day.

I tell him what
I learn in school.
And how I can reach
without a stool.

I draw him pictures
of Mom and me,
and of our house
and of the sea.

All the things I know
he misses,
and always I draw
lots of kisses.

I add a poem
that is a prayer:
God, keep him safe
way over there.

I draw some hearts
and then I sign
my first and last name
on the line.

My daddy—
he is far away.
I wish him home
most every day.

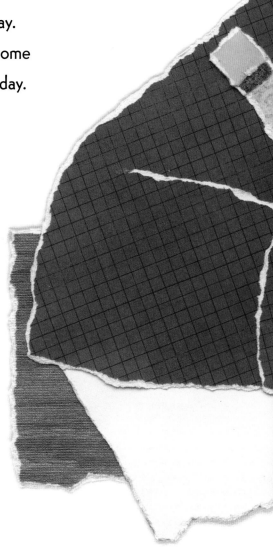

HAIRCUT

When it's time to cut my hair
I climb up on a kitchen chair
piled high with books to make me tall
but not so high that I could fall.

Daddy asks, "How would you like it?"
I smile big and say, "Please spike it!"
He wraps me in a backwards cape
to catch my hair when it escapes.

He tilts my head, my chin to chest.
And then his clippers do their best.
I can't hold still. I start to squirm.
I wiggle like a wiggly worm.

Then Daddy starts to wiggle, too.
We play this game till he is through.
"All done," he says, and helps me down.
"Now hit the road. Get out of town."
But I'll be back, because I know
my hair's already begun to grow!

DANCING

My daddy is a funny man.
Sometimes he will just take my hand
and ask me if I'd like to dance.
I say yes—I grab his pants
and carefully step on his feet.
Then we start moving to the beat.
When he steps left, I step there, too.
Then we step right—one, two, one, two.
Round and round the room I go,
holding tight to the best dad I know.
He picks me up. Gives me a spin.
The more we twirl, the more I grin.
The most fun that I've ever had
is going dancing with my dad.

DADDY!

Who tickles you and makes you laugh?
Daddy!
And when he has candy, who gives you half?
Daddy!

Who do you like? Who do you love?
Daddy!

Who do you wrestle? Who do you shove?
Daddy!

When he goes to work, who do you miss?
Daddy!

And when he comes home, who do you kiss?
Daddy!

Who says, "You can do it!" and makes you feel brave?
Daddy!

Who helps turn your bedroom into a bat cave?
Daddy!

Who shows you the world from the top of his head?
Daddy!

Who tells you a story and puts you to bed?
   Daddy!

      Who is your hero? Who's your very best friend?
         Daddy!

            Who says he loves you again and again?
               Daddy!

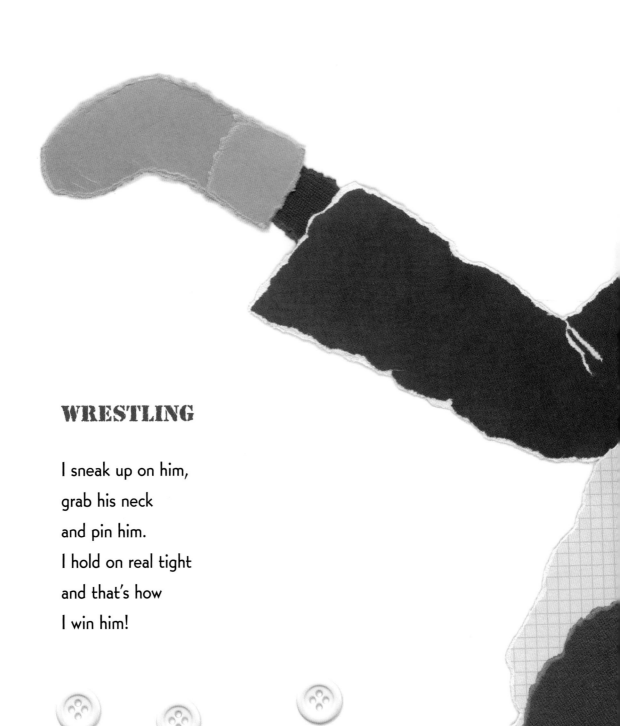

WRESTLING

I sneak up on him,
grab his neck
and pin him.
I hold on real tight
and that's how
I win him!

PLAYING CATCH

I'm playing catch out in the backyard,
but with just one person, it's kind of hard.
Dad promised he'd play when his work was all done,
but now sky is saying good night to the sun.
I know that he's busy . . . I was just hoping . . .
I try to hide it, but my face is moping.
The streetlights come on and silently call,
"Little children, come in now. The sun's getting small."
I throw my baseball up high in the air,
and when it comes down, my dad is right there.

THE GUITAR LESSON

If I'm extra special good
Daddy lets me play his guitar.
He makes me come real close,
places it gently in my hands.
"Hold it like a baby," Daddy says.
"Support its neck.
Treat it right and it'll sing to you."
I stand between Daddy's legs,
lean into him.
The up and down of his breathing
setting the tempo.
His heart beating out a rhythm.
I-love, this-boy, of-mine.
I-love, this-boy, of-mine.
My fingers strum the strings,
and the music wraps itself around us.
Daddy says, "Do you know this song?"
I smile and say, "It's called 'Our Family
in the Key of Happy.'"

LEARNING TO RIDE

I say good-bye to my old trike
and then I try my brand-new bike.
I hop on. Dad holds it steady.
A big thumbs-up
means that I'm ready.
"Don't let go," I say real soft.
"I'm afraid that I'll fall off."
I teeter, totter—I don't care—
because I know my dad's right there.
I pedal harder, we move faster.
My mom is watching,
we zoom right past her.
"Don't let go!" I start to scream.
"I won't," Dad says.
"We are a team."

Together, we go down my street,
Dad jogging as he holds my seat.
At first, we wobble. We keep trying
until it feels just like we're flying.

"Don't let go," I say again,
and Daddy says, "Go catch the wind."
I pedal and I chase the breeze.

The sun shines on me through the trees.

"You're doing it," I hear Dad say.

His voice sounds like it's far away.
And then I'm free, the wind is blowing,
my dad let go, but I'm still going!

REMEMBER THIS

Sometimes I forget
I'm supposed to be good.
I do what I want
and not what I should.
Then my daddy's voice
is as loud as the sea,
and I know I'm in trouble—
his words swallow me.
He's disappointed,
I'm sent to my room,
and all of his words
thunder and boom.
I feel really bad,
and my heart, it feels sore
'cause I'm thinking my best friend
don't like me no more.
Then Daddy comes in.
I look down at the ground.
His hand lifts my chin.
My heart starts to pound.

His eyes look at my eyes,
and his voice is real low.
He says, "Buddy, there's something
I want you to know.
Wherever you go
and whatever you do,
we'll always be best friends.
That will always be true."

SOME DADS

Some dads go to offices
and wear a suit and tie.
And some dads wear a uniform
and fly across the sky.
Some dads have a briefcase
full of all the work they do.
And some dads carry big long tubes
to hold the plans they drew.
Some dads work many hours
and get home late at night.
While some dads have to go to work
before it's even light.
Some dads go to meetings
and spend hours on the phone.
But my dad has the greatest job—
he's a dad that stays at home.

MY FIRST BOOK

My dad introduced me
to his favorite book,
and each night at bedtime
he reads while I look.

And now I have new friends
who live in the pages.
Dad says when we read
we free words from their cages.

Dad and I are readers.
We are word men, through and through.
I hope you have a dad like mine
who loves to read to you.

MY DADDY RULES THE WORLD

He helps me with my homework
and always gets it right.
He teaches me "most of the time,
it's better not to fight."
He drives me to my baseball game
and other games I play.
And best of all, no matter what,
he always wants to stay.
He knows the names of all my friends,
fist bumps and says, "My man."
He tells me that there is no "can't,"
there's only "yes, I can."
Whenever I have a problem,
he knows just what to do:
"In order to solve anything,
be honest, kind, and true."
My dad, he is a super man.
He doesn't need a cape
or the great big "S" I made
out of masking tape.
My daddy knows most everything
when his powers are unfurled,
and I'm not scared of anything—
my daddy rules the world.

This book is dedicated to dads, daddies, pops, and poppas.
To every man "fathering" a child and to those who stand in the
gap offering guidance, love, and support to children in need.
This book celebrates you.

Henry Holt and Company
Publishers since 1866
175 Fifth Avenue, New York, New York 10010
mackids.com

Henry Holt® is a registered trademark of Macmillan Publishing Group, LLC.
Copyright © 2017 by Hope Anita Smith. All rights reserved.
Photo in "Love Letter" is of Officer Anton Shufutinsky.

Library of Congress Cataloging-in-Publication Data is available.
ISBN 978-0-8050-9189-2

Our books may be purchased in bulk for promotional, educational, or business use.
Please contact your local bookseller or the Macmillan Corporate and Premium Sales Department at
(800) 221-7945 ext. 5442 or by e-mail at MacmillanSpecialMarkets@macmillan.com.

First Edition—2017 / Interior design by Patrick Collins
The artist used torn paper to create the illustrations for this book.
Printed in China by RR Donnelley Asia Printing Solutions Ltd., Dongguan City, Guangdong Province

1 3 5 7 9 10 8 6 4 2